Who's Afraid of ™

Spelling?

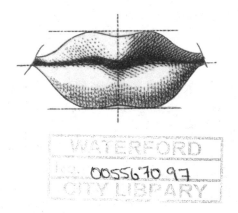

It's a damn poor mind that can think of only
one way to spell a word.

US President Andrew Jackson (1767–1845)

Editor: Stephen Haynes
Editorial assistant: Mark Williams

Published in Great Britain in MMXIV by
Book House, an imprint of
The Salariya Book Company Ltd
25 Marlborough Place, Brighton BN1 1UB
www.salariya.com
www.book-house.co.uk

HB ISBN-13: 978-1-909645-80-6

1 3 5 7 9 8 6 4 2

A CIP catalogue record for this book is available
from the British Library.
Printed and bound in China.
Printed on paper from sustainable sources.

Visit
www.salariya.com
for our online catalogue and
free interactive web books.

Who's Afraid of ™

Spelling?

> Which witch
> is which?

David Arscott

BOOK HOUSE
a SALARIYA imprint

I have often been obliged to sacrifice uniformity to custom; thus I write, in compliance with a numberless majority, *convey* and *inveigh*, *deceit* and *receipt*, *fancy* and *phantom*.

Dr Samuel Johnson, *Dictionary of the English Language* (1755)

My spelling is Wobbly. It's good spelling but it Wobbles, and the letters get in the wrong places.

A. A. Milne, *Winnie-the-Pooh*

Nanny Ogg knew how to start spelling 'banana', but didn't know how you stopped.

Terry Pratchett, *Witches Abroad*

I have been following the fate of the *h* in *rhubarb* in the Google database . . . In 2006 there were just a few hundred instances of *rubarb* . . . by the end of [2011] it had passed a million. If it carries on like this *rubarb* will overtake *rhubarb* as the commonest online spelling in the next five years.

David Crystal, *Spell It Out*

Contents

Preface

*I*N A TEXT to a friend you can write however you like, but there are some situations – such as applying for a job, or writing an essay or report – where you need to make a good impression on others. This book, and others in the series, will help you to write in a way that teachers, employers and others in authority will approve of.

What we describe here mainly applies to British English, although we do point out the most important differences between British and American usage. (Don't worry: there aren't nearly as many as you might imagine.) Commonwealth countries usually follow the British rules, with Canada drawing on both traditions.

Introduction

As she is spoke?

*F*OR NEWCOMERS to the language, written English can seem a terrible jumble. Some words that sound the same are spelled differently (*right, rite, write, wright*), some that look the same have different sounds (angry oarsmen may *row* as they *row* their boat), while others include letters which seem to be doing no useful work at all (the *b* in *debt*, the *h* in *rhyme*, the *s* in *island*, the *t* in *mortgage*).

Neither of the two obvious solutions to this problem is very appealing – that is, either to ferret endlessly through a dictionary or to learn every last spelling by heart. What we need are rules. The bad news is that the rules often clash. The good news is that understanding them can help fix difficult words in our memory banks.

First, let's explain (it may make you feel better) why our spelling has become such a minefield:

• There simply aren't enough letters to go round. We have 26 in our alphabet, but there are as many as 44 distinct sounds (or *phonemes*) recognised by language experts – 24 consonants and 20 vowels – and more than a million words to kit out with appropriate symbols.

• Language doesn't stand still. The earliest spelling system was the work of individual monks from the 7th century onwards, adapting the Germanic Anglo-Saxon vernacular to a Latin alphabet that, at the time, had only 23 letters. Over the following centuries spoken English changed immensely, and later scribes struggled manfully to make written sense of new sounds and a rapidly swelling vocabulary.

Ough dear!

'The baker gives a cough and then hiccoughs as his thorough fingers plough through the rough dough he bought' – eight different vowel sounds all represented by the same combination of four letters. It's enough to make you jump into the nearest lough!

• English has been enriched by words borrowed from languages around the world. While many (such as *alcohol*, *bandit* and *democracy*) have been given recognisably native dress, many others (*dahlia, pharaoh, spaghetti, verandah*) have been imported unchanged, giving them an exotic appearance – and making their spelling hard to remember.

• Dialect. Until southerners and northerners agree about how to say *bath*, the written form of that word (and a good many others) will have to represent two very different sounds.

Pedant alert!

Look out for our **PET PEEVE** symbol. There is a certain kind of person (language experts call them *peevologists*) who loves nothing better than to pick holes in other people's use of language. 'Pet peeves' are particular mistakes (or so-called mistakes) which cause these people to get dangerously steamed up and, in extreme cases, write letters to the papers in green ink.

This book is not meant to turn you into a peevologist yourself – perish the thought – but it could help you to avoid needlessly provoking such people.

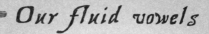

Our fluid vowels

Vowels are the sounds we make when we open our lips and keep our restless tongues away from our teeth and palates. On the page there are only five of them (a, e, i, o, u), plus y when it appears in words such as cry and gym – but you only have to exercise your vocal cords while gurning energetically (best done when alone) to realise what an impressive range of noises we can make.

Many words combine pairs of vowels in what are known as diphthongs (listen to the two distinct sounds in brown – 'bra-oon'), while others (such as flower) yoke three together as triphthongs ('fla-oo-uh'). Somehow the written language has to cope with this immense diversity.

English spelling, as we've noted, isn't entirely predictable, but an understanding of how words sound can often help fix them in your memory. Why do we write aim the way we do? Just listen to it, and you'll hear the two distinct vowel sounds – though, as we'll see in a minute, those sounds are not always represented by the same letters…

Here are eight distinct double-vowel sounds for you to experiment with: claim, deny, choice, below, owl, beard, their, your.

10

Making it long

One of the thorniest problems the Old English scribes had to face was how to distinguish long sounds from short. Say *fad* and *fade*, *hid* and *hide*, *cut* and *cute*, and you'll hear that the second of each pair has a more drawn-out (and also very different) vowel sound.

Now read the words and you'll be aware of one of the basic rules of English spelling – what schools used to teach as 'magic *e*' (nowadays it's called a split digraph). Add that letter to a simple one-syllable word ending in a consonant, and you effortlessly change the first vowel.

(Unfortunately, it doesn't follow that such sounds are always written with the same combination of letters. We don't write *dide*, for instance. This is because we're using the past tense of the verb *to die*, and we spell it *died* (*die* + *d*) to show how the two words are related.)

A second way of marking a longer sound is to place two vowel letters together before the

11

final consonant, as in *boat, cheap* and *maid*. We don't double up *a, i* or *u*, except in a handful of imported words, but we're all familiar with a wide range of *ee* and *oo* words. In fact, the scribes who helped fix the language were so fond of this convention that single-syllable words spelt with *ee* (*deed, feed, need; feel, kneel, reel* and so on) are much more common than those that use the split digraph (such as *eve*).

The *oo* words usually have a similar lengthening effect, but read this selection out loud: *blood, boot, door, good, school*. If you're a speaker of RP English (that is, Received Pronunciation, sometimes called BBC English), those vowels represent five different sounds. Why? Well, they all sounded very much alike hundreds of years ago, but over many generations the spoken language has changed faster than the written language.

Pet peeve And by the way...

Do please note a vital difference between the two words *pronounce* and *pronunciation*. There's little that annoys the language purist more than to catch someone either writing or saying 'pronounciation' – in their critical eyes, it announces that you're a dunce!

Keeping it short

We've seen that single vowels in one-syllable words are short, but how do we keep them that way in a longer word? Easy! Just as a double vowel gives a long sound, so a double consonant creates a short one. This, thankfully, is another common spelling rule, and it's one that most of us understand without even thinking about it.

If, for example, we wish to write about the sheets and blankets on a *bed*, we spell the word *bedding*. There isn't a common word 'beding', but we know full well that if it did exist we would pronounce it to rhyme with 'beading', giving it a long vowel. In similar fashion, *cap* proceeds to *capping*, *vet* to *vetting* and so on.

Spelling trivia

Britain's only venomous snake was the nadder, *but because everyone heard it as 'an adder', that became the usual form. The same happened with the* napron.

13

There are, of course, a few exceptions to the rule. Although *bet* gives us *betting*, *sweat* becomes *sweating* on account of the two vowels before the *t*. Yes, this seems illogical, but in Old English the *ea* was probably sounded as a diphthong.

Orrm wrestling

Late in the 12th century, a monk writing a biblical verse commentary in his Lincolnshire monastery made a valiant attempt to produce a written English which exactly reproduced the sounds he heard all around him. The monk's name was Orrm, we know his work as the Orrmulum – *and unhappily his ingenious language system was doomed to failure.*

*Linguists value the book because it gives them a clear idea of how the East Midlands dialect sounded at the time. Unfortunately it contains features his successors found too fussy, including accent marks (diacritics) to show where words were stressed. Orrm was an advocate of the double consonant to indicate a short preceding vowel, but his zealous use of it in every single case (*affterr, dogg, Ennglissh*) would have been time-consuming for a scribe and wasteful of a printer's ink. He had wrestled manfully with the maddening English language, and lost.*

Awkward add-ons

Things get more complicated when we bolt extra bits onto the front and back of words. These are called 'affixes', and there are two kinds. We set off to *camp*, for instance, and make an *encampment*. In this case, *camp* is the 'stem' of the word, *en-* is a prefix and *-ment* is a suffix.

Prefixes

There are quite a few prefixes in English, among them *a-*, *ab-*, *co-*, *com-*, *con-*, *dis-*, *en-*, *im-*, *in-*, *mis-*, *pre-*, *pro-*, *re-*, *trans-* and *un-*. Most of these can be attached to the front of the word stem without a second thought: *enslave, inconsiderate, unfrock*.

The head-scratching begins with words that might or might not have a double letter in them. *Immodest* is straightforward because the *im-* prefix is attached to the familiar *modest*, but what about *abbreviate* and *aberrant*? Alas, you need to know that the former comes from the Latin *ab-breviare* (where the second *b* is part of the stem), the latter from *ab-errare* (whose stem does not have a *b*).

15

Similarly, that perennial (Latin *per-ennis*) look-up word *commemorate* derives from the Latin *com-memorare* and its partner-in-crime *accommodate* from *ad-commodare* (with the *d* changed to match the following letter, as often happens in Latin).

Sometimes a prefix ending with *s* is followed by a stem word beginning with the same letter. As a rule, the double *s* is fine (*assail, dissect*), but when the *s* of the stem word is followed by a consonant, you drop the extra *s* (*trans* + *spire* gives *transpire*). You'd like an exception? *Misspell*!

Suffixes

With suffixes we find ourselves on much thornier ground. For one thing, there are so many more of them. For another, the lengthening of a word brought about by a suffix (or a string of suffixes, as in *pain/painful/painfully*) can change not only the word stress and the vowel sound, but (as we've seen with *pronounce/pronunciation*) even the spelling of the original stem word.

Suffixes that begin with a consonant (*-ful, -less, -ly, -ment, -ness, -tion, -ward*) can often be tagged on just as they are: *thankful, tireless, contentment* and the like. Does this seem too good to be true?

16

It is, because many more begin with a vowel, among them this little collection: *-able, -acy, -age, -ance, -ant, -ate, -ence, -ently, -er, -ible, -ic, -ify, -ing, -ise, -ish, -ism, -ist, -ity, -ive, -or, -our, -ous, -ual, -y.* It often feels rather hit-and-miss pinning these tails on the stem-word donkey, so we need a few rules to prevent us blundering about blindfold.

• When the stem word ends with a short vowel, you will need to 'protect' its status by following the double-consonant rule: *remit/remittance, upset/upsetting.*

BUT you won't need any doubling if the stem word contains two vowels (*fool/foolish, leaf/leafy, shout/shouting*) or ends with more than one consonant: (*bend/bending, match/matching*).

• Stress plays an important role in English pronunciation. Note how you double the consonant to keep the vowel short when the stress falls on the last syllable of the stem word: *confer/conferred/conferring, underpin/underpinned/underpinning.*

BUT you should leave a single consonant when the emphasis falls on an earlier syllable, as in *open/opened/opening, focus/focused/focusing, proffer/proffered/proffering.*

17

• If the original word ends in an *e* you usually drop it: *cure/curable, fame/famous, force/forcing.*

BUT there are (of course) some exceptions, among them *agreeable, mileage* and (optionally) *likeable* – plus an array of words which follow the 'famous/evil' rule on the facing page.

• The *-sion, -tion* suffixes can be confusing. If the stem word ends in *d* or *s* you generally use the former (*extend/extension, suppress/suppression*), while (logically, you may think) a *t* sound at the end usually demands the latter: *complete/completion.*

BUT there's an exception with the *-mit* stem, which gives us *commit/commission, omit/omission.*

• In UK (but not US) English, a suffix added to a word ending in *l* has that letter doubled: *fulfil/fulfilled/fulfilling, travel/travelled/travelling.*

• Change the *ou* in words ending in *-our* (*humour*) to *o* (*humorous*) before the suffixes *-ary, -ation, -ific, -ious, -is, -itic, -ise* and *ous.* Otherwise, leave things as they are (*colourful*).

• When adding an *-ing* ending to a verb ending in *ie*, drop those two letters and replace them with *y*: *die/dying, lie/lying, tie/tying.*

18

Famous hard men, evil softies

If you're familiar with any of the 'Romance' languages (the modern European languages descended from Latin), you'll recognise an annoying confusion they share with us over the pronunciation of the letters c *and* g *before a vowel. The early scribes who helped shape the written language realised that the sounds emerging from their lips when making* a, o *and* u *sounds at the back of their throats were different from those they produced when pursing their lips to form* e *and* i *at the front.*

Unfortunately they used the same letters for both, leaving us to cope with 'hard' sounds in cap, cop, cup, gap, got *and* gut *(the vowels in 'famous') and 'soft' ones in* cep, civic, gender *and* giblets *(the vowels in 'evil'). Oh, and we should throw in* cynic *and* gym *here, too.*

True, a hard g *appears at the front of words such as* gift *and* gig *– and a very surprising soft* g *in* gaol *– but the 'famous/evil' rule applies in most cases, and it affects how you manage suffixes attached to a stem word ending in* e. *In order to preserve the soft sound, you have to retain that final 'e':* changeable, courageous, manageable, noticeable, outrageous, peaceable.

• In words ending *–ay*, *-ey*, *-oy* or *-uy*, keep the *y* when adding *-ed*, *-er* and *-ing* endings: *buy/buyer/buying, destroy/destroyed/ destroying, play/player/played/playing* and *survey/ surveyed/surveying*.

BUT beware that the likes of *dry/drying* and *pry/ prying* seem to follow this rule, only to deceive. The clue is that they have no vowel before the *y*, and their past tenses are *dried* and *pried* – usefully distinct from the deadly sin of *pride*.

Neither one nor the other

What's the most common vowel sound in English? Schwa! That's how linguists describe the vague 'uh' sound we let fall from our lips in the unstressed parts of vast numbers of words. It's another reason spelling is so difficult: those indistinct little sounds don't give you a proper clue about which vowel to write down.

• Get rid of a final *y*, on the other hand, and replace it with *i*, in combinations such as *beauty/ beautiful, busy/busily, dreamy/dreaminess, eighty/ eightieth, lazy/laziness, multiply/multiplied, mystery/ mysterious*. In plurals, change *y* to *ie*: *baby/babies, duty/duties, lorry/lorries*.

A final tip about getting to know words which change their vowels once they have suffixes dangling from them: see if you can work out how the word has been put together. Faced with writing *typical* you might, if not familiar with it, wonder whether to put an *i* in the first syllable – after all, that's what it sounds like – but if you know that its stem is *type*, you'll be pretty confident about spelling it with a *y*.

Pet peeve

As for *definitely*, it's extremely useful to know that it comprises the word *finite* with a *de-* prefix and a *-ly* suffix. Why? Because otherwise you might be horribly tempted, as so many people are, to write 'definately' – high in the peevologists' top ten of horrors.

The reason for the mistake isn't hard to find: take a look at the box on the facing page. Because the stress of the word is at the beginning, the *n*t* syllable at its core becomes a blurry 'schwa' sound. It could be filled with any of the five vowels and the human ear wouldn't pick up the difference. Is this a persuasive argument for getting to know how the language works in order to be able to spell it well? Definitely!

Eatable edibles

How on earth do you work out whether to give adjectives like these an -able or -ible ending? After all, they both use the 'schwa' vowel, which makes them indistinguishable when spoken aloud.

A linguist might have the advantage of knowing which of them come from either the Latin -abilis or -ibilis, or the French -able or -ible, but most of us can be forgiven for not having a clue about such niceties.

Here are a few useful tips:

• *The vast majority of these almost identical twins end in* -able, *so it's a good idea to choose that ending if you have to make a guess.*

• *If the stem is a self-contained word (such as* eat, above, *as opposed to* ed-*) it's much more likely to end in* -able. *(*Capable, durable *and* equable *are among the few you'd therefore expect to be* -ible *words, but aren't.)*

• *Put an* e *before the* -able *ending if you need to keep a soft* c *or* g*:* changeable, manageable, peaceable, traceable. *But don't use an* e *before* -ible.

Here's a checklist of our Top 50 -ible endings:

accessible

audible

collapsible

combustible

compatible

comprehensible

contemptible

convertible

credible

crucible

defensible

digestible

discernible

edible

eligible

fallible

feasible

flexible

forcible

fungible

gullible

horrible

inadmissible

incorrigible

incorruptible

indelible

indestructible

indivisible

inexhaustible

inexpressible

intelligible

invincible

irascible

irrepressible

legible

negligible

ostensible

perceptible

permissible

plausible

possible

reducible

reprehensible

responsible

reversible

sensible

susceptible

tangible

terrible

visible

I before e . . .

And now for another of those throwbacks to the classrooms of yesteryear, in which millions of us were instructed to chant:

I before *e*, except after *c*.

The idea was to din into our young brains the fact that words such as *achieve, belief, chief* and (appropriately) *grief* had the *ie* rather than the *ei* spelling, whereas *ceiling, deceive* and *receipt* sported the letters the other way round.

These days, there's a widespread criticism of this memory rhyme on the basis that it doesn't allow for all the exceptions to the rule – which reminds us that there was often a second line to learn, which ran:

Unless it sounds *eh* as in *neighbour* and *weigh*.

The critics are right about the many exceptions, but they're surely missing the point – just as that second rhyme does.

24

Once you admit *neighbour* and *weigh* as being outside the frame, you start to find a host of other 'rule-breakers' – plurals, which change words such as *agency* and *lunacy* to *agencies* and *lunacies*; comparatives such as *lacier* and *racier*; past tenses such as *fancied*; and suffixes such as the one that changes *suffice* to *sufficient*.

But let's return to the schoolroom. The basic lesson, after all, was simply meant to apply to commonly used words that contain the 'ee' sound. And it works! Confine yourself to those and you need only trouble yourself with a handful of irregulars, of which we'd highlight three: *seize, weir* and *weird*.

Sometimes the experts are too clever by half.

Spelling trivia

Can you see what these words have in common?

abstemiously
adventitiously
facetiously

All contain the five vowels in alphabetical order – with a y *at the end for good measure.*

Saxon echoes

It's time for a little Anglo-Saxon archaeology – of the verbal kind, of course. We'll begin by saying a few words out loud and discovering what they have in common:

acknowledge
breakneck
Cockney

The answer is that double *kn*-sound in the middle. We create the first part of it by raising our tongue to the soft palate and releasing it to let the air escape. (Try it!) For the second part we swiftly raise the tongue to the top of the mouth just behind our teeth, again releasing it to make the sound.

It's over in a fraction of a second, and we normally think nothing of it – 'Can I canoe you down the river?' closely echoes the sequence – but we're not used to starting a word that way. But that's what the Anglo-Saxons did, just as Germans still do today.

You'd need a primer to make sense of those Anglo-Saxon writings of more than a thousand years ago, but you can make a reasonable stab at reading their words aloud once you know that every letter was sounded.

Their word for understanding something was *cnawan*, and you can probably work out how that shifted to become a familiar word today. One clue is that later scribes changed the *c* at the front to a *k*. Yes, with a shift in the vowel the Old English word became our *know* – and of course we no longer sound the first consonant.

Here are a few other *cn* openers that have come down to us today:

cnaedan	to knead
cneow	knee
cnif	knife
cnight	knight
cnocian	to knock
cnotta	knot
cnyttan	to knit

Although there are *kn*-words in the dictionary *without* an Old English origin, knowing where the above come from should help to fix their spellings in your mind. And the same applies to some other consonantal doubles, or digraphs.

For instance, the *gn* sound we're familiar with in *ignorant* and *agnostic* was once sounded in such words as *gnat* and *gnaw*. (No, *gnu* isn't an English word, and as far as we know – and despite Flanders and Swann – the initial *g* was never pronounced.)

And take the words *answer* and *sword*. Strange to say, the *w* was indeed given its full value all those centuries ago.

A queer fish

The playwright George Bernard Shaw (1856–1950) was a fervent advocate of spelling reform and left money in his will for the creation of a new set of 40 letter shapes to represent the sounds of the language. An edition of his play Androcles and the Lion *was eventually published by Penguin, with the text in both conventional and Shavian characters, but the system never caught on.*

Shaw liked to taunt his opponents by telling them that the letters ghoti *spelled 'fish' –* gh *as in* enough, *i as in* women, *and* ti *as in* nation. *Of course, no English word beginning in* gh *has the* f *sound there and no word ends in* ti *to sound* sh, *but he'd made his point.*

Perhaps the largest group of these historic throw-backs is the one comprising *wr* words. *Writan* has undergone a very small change to become our *write*, while a few show no orthographic change at all. Here's a selection for you:

wraec	wrack (as in 'wrack and ruin')
wraestlung	wrestling
wraethu	wrath (anger)
wrecan	to wreak (as in havoc)
wrecca	wretch
wrenna	wren
wrist	wrist
writ	writ
writhan	to writhe
wrong	wrong

Hwaet!

And then there's that strange class of mainly questioning words that begin with *wh* – *who, what, why, where, when* – but don't seem to have any use for the *h* at all. The thing to understand here is that these were once written with the two letters the other way around, as in the opening word of the great poem *Beowulf* and many another Old English work: 'Hwaet!'

It's the equivalent of our word *what*, although when Anglo-Saxon poets used it at the opening of a public performance it had more the sense of 'Now take a listen to this, folks!'

The point is that the initial *h* really did represent a sound made ahead of the *w* – and it's one you can still hear on the tongues of some English (and many Scottish) speakers today. Here are a few Anglo-Saxon forms and their modern equivalents:

hwa/hwas	who/whose
hwaael	whale
hwaem	whom
hwaenne	when
hwaer	where
hwilc	which
hwistle	whistle
hwit	white

But how did those initial letters come to be reversed? Because as time went by there were so many other digraphs where the *h* came second (*ch*, *gh*, *sh* and *th*) that *hwo, hwaet* and *hwere* seemed nothing short of outlandish. By a process of analogy – that is, finding a similarity between unconnected things – they were quietly reordered, the better to fit into polite orthographic society. Hwaet a shame!

The most famous date in English history is 1066, when William the Conqueror's French-speaking Norman forces overcame King Harold at the Battle of Hastings. The defeated Saxons had worse things to worry about than the effect on their language, but over a relatively short space of time English itself was infiltrated by a swarming army of newly coined words – and our spelling bears the consequences of it today.

The language (spoken and written) that developed from 1066 until around 1400 is known as Middle English. Compare an Old English text such as *Beowulf* with the *Canterbury Tales* of Geoffrey Chaucer (c.1343–1400) and you'll be struck by how readable the later work is by comparison. That's because many – though far from all – of the spelling conventions we accept today had already been adopted by the scribes charged not only with penning religious tracts and works of literature, but also with drawing up legal documents and archives for the state.

31

They had problems from the start. The Anglo-Saxon scholars they replaced had been using some strange-looking symbols unknown to their Latin script, including two ('thorn' and 'eth') which denoted the different varieties of the *th* sound in words such as *thought* and *them*. The Norman scribes immediately discarded all of these, and then had to decide how to adapt their alphabet to what was for them a completely new vocabulary.

The problem only worsened as a host of new words entered the language century by century. First the newcomers imported their own Norman French usages – some replacing English words, others introducing new concepts to the island's inhabitants.

Gourmet grub

*The Anglo-Saxons ate the animals they farmed, of course, and they left us their names for them, but it was the French who gave us the words we use for the cooked joints. We raise pigs for pork (*porc*), calves for veal (*veau*), cows for beef (*bœuf*) and sheep for mutton (*mouton*) – but, no, we have no specialised word for horsemeat.*

Then there were the many borrowings from Latin, the *lingua franca* of all European scholars in the Middle Ages, and yet more – as the Renaissance brought new learning to the continent – from Greek.

Throw in new coinages resulting from trade around the globe, and these scribes had their work cut out to adapt their limited alphabet to represent such a vast array of sounds in a logical system. Unhappily, they mixed and matched their various stratagems so haphazardly that we have to work hard to find useful rules for them.

Verbal genetics

For instance, although the scribes generally respected the double-consonant rule for short vowels (page 13), they attached an equal importance to honouring the origins of words. You might have expected the Latin *spiritus* to become 'spirrit', but we know it as *spirit* – and we now accept it alongside rather too many other short-vowel derivations such as *acid, habit, closet, comet* and *solid*. You just have to learn them.

Conversely, Latin does give us a double consonant in words like *horrid* and *pallid*, while *ferrule/ferule* can be spelt either way. Grr!

Crazy consonants

Just like the five vowels, our 21 consonant letters are employed individually and in combination to represent a wide array of sounds. Here are just a few examples:

ch

c *is found in some foreign imports:* cello, ciao
The ch *digraph can go anywhere:* church, lecher
t *(pronounced like* ch *in some varieties of English) goes in the middle:* mature, nature
tch *goes only at the end of a syllable:* itch, watch

k

c *has this sound before an* a, o *or* u: can, cod, cud *and, rarely, an* e: Celtic
ch *anywhere:* chaos, lachrymose, stomach
ck *anywhere but the beginning:* ticker, clock
k *anywhere:* key, basket, cook
kk *rarely:* trekked
qu *at the beginning, middle or near the end:* quay, conquer, discotheque

j

dg *or* dge *in the middle or at the end:* badger, judge, judgment/judgement

g *before* e *and* i, *and very rarely before* a: gem, giant, gaol

j *anywhere:* jewel, banjo, raj

f

f *anywhere, though at the end of a word it may signify a* v *sound:* fat, before, whereof

ff *in the middle or at the end:* differ, quiff

gh *never at the front as an* f *sound:* rough, tougher

ph *anywhere:* physio, graphic, nephew, cenotaph

sh

ce *in the middle:* ocean

ch *anywhere:* chute, marchioness, louche

sh *in any position:* ship, cushion, finish

ssi *only in the middle:* passion

ssu *only in the middle:* pressure

ti *only in the middle:* motion, portion, ration

zh

j *in foreign loan words:* bijou, raj *(sometimes)*

si *in the middle:* decision

su *in the middle:* measure, closure

zu *in the middle:* azure, measure

A similar 'rule' applies to the spelling of *abolish* and *punish* with a single consonant, yet *doggish* and *mannish* with two: the latter pair come from Old English adjectives, the former from French verbs. Their 'genetic' backgrounds likewise explain the otherwise illogical *leper/pepper* and *proper/copper* inconsistencies.

Dubious derivations

What now seems the craziest idea of all was mucking about with perfectly good words in order to reveal their antecedents. That strange word *doubt* was originally spelled *doutte* (among various other forms), but later scribes thought it would be helpful to remind readers of its origins in the Latin word *dubitum*, so they stuck the *b* in.

Shakespeare's pedantic, and therefore ludicrous, Holofernes in *Love's Labours Lost* laments the fact that people fail to pronounce the *l* in *calf* and *half* and the *b* in *doubt* and *debt*. Sensible people never had done. Yes, there had been a perfectly acceptable *dette* at one time, too, but the Latin *debitum* was raided for its telltale letter. This maddening practice has deformed many of the words we most fear to spell, among them *indict*, *receipt* and *subtle*. In some cases (*assault*, *fault*) the extra letter has since come to be pronounced.

The infiltrated letter is a *mnemonic*, a device to aid the memory. This word itself has a silent *m* at the front (from the Greek this time) – and you can find a catalogue of hush-hush letters by turning the page.

Note, by the way, that if a peevologist attempts to crush you for spelling the word *Arctic* without the first *c*, you can point out with a little sneer that it was orginally spelled *Artik*. Pronunciation (this would have delighted Holofernes) later changed to fit the spelling, just as it did with *assault* and *fault*.

Pet peeve

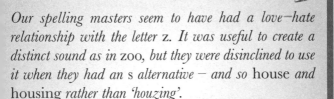

Whoreson zed

Our spelling masters seem to have had a love–hate relationship with the letter z. *It was useful to create a distinct sound as in* zoo, *but they were disinclined to use it when they had an* s *alternative – and so* house *and* housing *rather than 'houzing'.*

True, it was rather laborious to write on the page, but there seems to have been a more widespread dislike of it. In Shakespeare's King Lear, *Kent berates the steward Oswald: 'Thou whoreson zed! Thou unnecessary letter!'*

Dumbing down

Most of the consonants appear as silent letters from time to time, and here's a clutch of these spellers' nightmares:

b   *aplomb, bomb, climb, comb, crumb, debt, doubt, dumb, jamb, lamb, limb, numb, plumb, subtle, succumb, thumb, tomb, womb*

c   *abscess, ascend, ascent, crescent, descend, descent, disciple, fascinate, fluorescent, incandescent, isosceles, luminescent, miscellaneous, muscle, obscene, resuscitate, scenario, scene, scent, scissors, scythe*

ch *chthonic*

d   *handkerchief, sandwich, Wednesday*

g   *align, assign, benign, campaign, champagne, cologne, consign, design, feign, foreign, gnarl, gnash, gnat, gnaw, gnome, gnu, phlegm, reign, resign, sign*

gh *night (and many similar* -ight *forms)*

h   *ache, anchor, archaeology, architect, archives, chaos, character, charisma, chemical, chlorine, choir, cholera, chord, choreograph, chorus, Christian, chrome, diarrhoea, echo, exhaust, exhume, heir, honest, hour, khaki, leprechaun, mechanic, melancholy, monarch, monochrome, nihilist, orchestra, orchid, philharmonic, physic, psychic, scheme, school, silhouette, stomach, technology, Thames*

38

k *knack, knapsack, knave, knead, knee, knell, knickers, knife, knight, knit, knob, knock, knoll, knot, know, knuckle*

l *calf, half, palm, could, should, would*

m *mnemonic*

n *autumn, column, condemn, damn, hymn, solemn*

p *corps, coup, pneumonia, psychology, pseudonym, ptarmigan, pterodactyl, receipt*

ph *phthisis*

r *barn, farther, iron (in some varieties of English)*

s *fracas, island, isle, viscount*

t *apostle, ballet, bristle, bustle, castle, fasten, glisten, gourmet, gristle, hustle, jostle, listen, moisten, mortgage, often, ostler, nestle, rapport, ricochet, rustle, soften, thistle, trestle, whistle, wrestle*

th *asthma, isthmus*

w *answer, awry, gunwale, playwright, sword, two, who, whole, wrack, wrangle, wrap, wrath, wreak, wreath, wreck, wren, wrench, wrest, wrestle, wretch, wriggle, wring, wrinkle, wrist, writ, write, writhe, wrong, wrought, wrung, wry*

x *faux*

z *rendezvous*

Two famously difficult surnames: Cholmondley (pronounced Chumley), Featherstonehaugh (Fanshaw). Two placenames: Leicester (Lester), Bicester (Bister).

Getting it wrong

If it makes you feel any better, we should point out that these fussy etymologists – the earnest scribes who believed that they should mimic the origins of words in creating their English versions – often got things wrong. Here are a few of their lulus. (A word they didn't know, of course.)

Hiccough
You are allowed to spell it *hiccup*, which is how it sounds and always did, more or less. What happened here isn't difficult to work out. The embarrassing little oral explosion sounds something like a soprano *cough*, and the spelling was changed to match it.

Could do better

It's such a familiar word that we're unlikely to misspell it, but could *shouldn't really have that silent l in it. In Anglo-Saxon times it was pronounced rather like* coother. *The two similar words* sholde *and* wolde *became* should *and* would *– and, by the process of analogy,* could *was given the same treatment.*

Island

The Old English word derived from *ey* – as in the place name Pevensey – meaning an area of land surrounded by water, and it was commonly written as *iland* or *igland*. It later became confused with the Old French word *ile*, which itself was given a silent *s* on the grounds that its Latin original was *insula*. Once the *isle* spelling caught on it was inevitable that *island* would be dragged into the same messy business. Do put it in – but feel free to curse under your breath.

Ptarmigan

The Scottish bird is better known for that silent *p* at the front than for anything else, and it really shouldn't be there. One of the early spellings was *termagent*, which would have suited it (and us) just fine. Unfortunately, it was for some reason thought to have Greek origins, like *pterodactyl*, and the rest is spelling history.

Scissors

In this case there was a muddle between two possible Latin precursors. The correct one was *cisorium*, a cutting implement – and if they'd got it right we would happily be writing 'cissors'. *Un*happily, scholars thought the word came from *scindere* (to cut), and the *sc* proved irresistible.

41

Agonising endings

It's because of those Latin and French origins that we have so many endings that sound the same but require a different treatment. Take a look at these pairs of adjectives:

facial	palatial
official	initial
laughable	risible

There are many more like these and no, of course you can't be expected to know their derivations. Although the *-able/-ible* tips on pages 22–23 should help, you simply have to familiarise yourself with them.

Verbs ending in *-ise* and *-ize* are another minefield. Knowing that the former came from the French and the latter from Greek via Latin isn't going to help most of us, but in this area we can at least offer a little positive help. British English generally favours *-ise* rather than *-ize*, although a dictionary will show you that we can both *agonise* and *agonize* over the matter. US English always goes for the *z* spelling.

But there are a number of verbs which *must* be spelled with an *s*; the *z* option is not available because the *s* belongs to the stem of the verb, not the ending. Here's our Top Twenty:

advertise	exercise
advise	franchise
apprise	improvise
chastise	incise
circumcise	merchandise
comprise	revise
compromise	supervise
despise	surmise
devise	surprise
excise	televise

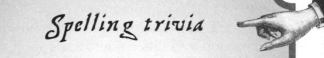

Spelling trivia

• Queueing *is the only English word which has five vowels in a row.*

• Bookkeeper *is the only word containing three double letters in a row.*

• Asthma *is the only six-letter word that begins and ends with a vowel and has no other vowels between.*

Fine distinctions

Often the scribes gave different spellings to words that sound the same (see the section beginning on page 50). Their use of the *-ice* and *-ise* endings to distinguish nouns from verbs has given us the following (though not all of these examples hold in American English):

Noun	*Verb*
advice	advise
device	devise
licence	license
practice	practise
prophecy	prophesy

Some of these pairs (*advice/advise*, *device/devise*) are easier to remember because they are pronounced differently. This is good news, as you can use *advice/advise* as a mnemonic to help you remember the others.

I'd like someone to *advise* me, because I'm always willing to act on good *advice*.

The authorities only *license* good restaurants, and I've had my *licence* for thirty years.

Practice makes perfect – so let's start to *practise*!

The Great Vowel Shift

If you've ever watched a newsreel from the 1950s you'll know that English accents have changed over the years, the upper classes in those days pronouncing the word house *almost as if it were 'hice'. The sounds we make aren't fixed – and the biggest change ever occurred during the two centuries from around 1400, a process known as the Great Vowel Shift.*

For reasons we can only guess at, the long vowels began to be spoken further towards the front of the mouth, and as one vowel pushed up against another with a similar sound, that vowel in turn was 'raised' (pronounced with the tongue higher in the mouth) to make room for it.

Our spelling often reveals what happened. Why do children *and* child *use the same five letters although we hear them differently? Because the former has an (unchanged) short vowel and the latter a long vowel, raised from something like 'chilled' to the sound we know today. The* ou *in* loud *tells us that it was once pronounced 'lood', the* i *in* wipe *reflects its earlier sound of 'weep', and* leaf *once chimed roughly with 'lay off'. More complications!*

Ghastly ghosts

William Caxton set up the first printing press in England in the 1470s, and you might imagine that the stream of books he produced would have helped settle the notoriously fickle English spelling once and for all. In fact, Caxton – a merchant and diplomat, as well as an author and printer – seems not to have regarded the standardisation of the language as a priority, and he left much of the detail to his compositors, several of them (including the best-known, Wynkyn de Worde) hailing from the Low Countries.

It's these Flemish collaborators we have to thank for a few of our more outlandish spellings. Why the h in ghost, which the Anglo-Saxons were perfectly happy to read as goost? Because Caxton's Netherlandish collaborators had their own word gheest, and it therefore seemed a good idea to them to put the h in.

They did the same with aghast and ghastly, and it was inevitable that when ghoul (an Arabic word) came into the language it should have the same digraph planted at the front. And then in came a new kind of cucumber needing an English name: welcome the gherkin!

Dr Johnson prescribes

The French and the Italians formed Academies to pronounce on the correct use of their languages, and as the printed word spread in the 17th and 18th centuries there were calls for the English to follow suit. It never happened, perhaps because that kind of logical top-down approach was alien to the native temperament.

What we did have was a one-man academy in the bulky form of the learned Dr Samuel Johnson. Truth to say, English spelling had pretty well settled down by the time he came on the scene, but his *Dictionary of the English Language*, published in 1755, satisfied the keenly felt need for lexical authority. His prodigious work would soon be on the shelves of practically every literate or would-be literate family in the land.

As we saw on page 4, Johnson accepted very many of the spellings he found in common use, arguing that 'it is more important for a law to be known than for it to be right'.

'Dictionaries,' he said, 'are like watches: the worst is better than none, and the best cannot be expected to go quite true.'

Where he had to make a choice between two forms, he often took into account the origins of the word: 'I write *enchant, enchantment, enchanter*, after the French, and *incantation* after the Latin; thus *entire* is chosen rather than *intire*, because it passed to us not from the Latin *integer*, but from the French *entier*.'

He had his critics, but Lord Chesterfield spoke for many when he wrote that he happily bent the knee to the doctor on these matters: 'I hereby declare that I make a total surrender of all my rights and privileges in the English language, as a freeborn British subject, to the said Mr Johnson during the term of his dictatorship.'

Not all of his strategies have stood the test of time (he preferred a final *k* in *critick* and *musick*, for example), but his dictionary was superior to its predecessors both in giving examples of words as they appeared in literature – there were more than 100,000 quotations in all – and in its meticulousness. His 43,000 entries included 16 definitions of the word *turn*, 20 of *time* and no fewer than 123 of *take*.

He was often pompous (he thought words such as *bang, budge, fuss* and *shabby* too 'low' to include), but could be humorous, too. Here are four of his memorable definitions:

Excise: a hateful tax levied upon commodities and adjudged not by the common judges of property but wretches hired by those to whom excise is paid.

Lexicographer: a writer of dictionaries; a harmless drudge that busies himself in tracing the original and detailing the signification of words.

Monsieur: a term of reproach for a Frenchman.

Oats: a grain which in England is generally given to horses, but in Scotland supports the people.

Johnson's was the standard work until the publication between 1884 and 1928 of the *Oxford English Dictionary* (which at first included some 1,700 of his definitions, marking them with a 'J'). Today's *OED* is for many the supreme authority as regards spelling and usage – but of course the English language refuses to be tamed and is ever-changing.

Dangerous doubles

English is awash with homophones – words which sound the same but have different meanings. When they have different spellings, too (*allowed/aloud*), they present a tough challenge to the unwary. In this chapter we bring you the trickiest of them in contexts which should help distinguish them in your memory.

They often come in pairs, hence the title of this chapter, but you'll find quite a few rhyming triplets, too. Beware!

The bride tripped up on her walk to the *altar*. Next time she would *alter* the length of her dress.

She thought her husband had an *aural* [ear] problem because he never heard a word she said. He thought she had an *oral* [mouth] problem, because she talked too much.

They spent the morning shopping in the *bazaar*, and bought some *bizarre* ethnic wind chimes.

50

They spent the day swimming from the *beach*, which was overhung by a large *beech* tree.

He died after eating an exotic *berry*, and they had to *bury* him many miles from home.

The ship was moored in its *berth* at the quayside, where the captain's wife gave *birth* to twins.

He had no idea what to *buy* for the babies. *By* chance he found the ideal shop, run by a helpful *bi*sexual, who called '*Bye!*' as he left.

She would like to have been *bolder* than she was. Her timidity was like a huge *boulder* that blocked her path.

When the hand*brake* failed, the car crashed. The driver, who had been taking a *break*, rushed to stop it and managed to *break* his leg.

The baker sold mouldy *bread*, but the customer was too well-*bred* to complain.

He had a secret *cache* of weapons, which he never meant to use. He wouldn't part with it, however much *cash* you offered.

A historian claimed that Nelson's *cannon* [guns] fired roast potatoes at the French fleet.
Nobody believed this, as his book wasn't part of the *canon* [body of writings considered genuine or trustworthy].

Jackson Pollock liked to throw paint at his *canvas*.
A *canvass* [survey] of public opinion suggested that this was rather excessive.

What on earth is that mess on the *ceiling*?
It's a Pollock lookalike for *sealing* the cracks.

The prisoner's *cell* attracted a large crowd as he had narcotics to *sell*.

Young Charlie tipped his *cereal* bowl over the floor yet again – he was a *serial* [repeat] offender.

The songbird was going very *cheap*, because the only sound it could manage was a pathetic *cheep*.

The *Czech* gentleman went into the bank to *check* his balance.
The problem was that his *cheque* had bounced.

The sailor's language was horribly *coarse*.
His companions were glad when he returned to his boat and set *course* for distant lands.

Shrugging his shoulders in a *complacent* manner often got Steve in trouble for not bothering. His sister Ruby, on the other hand, was far too *complaisant* – always willing to please.

Three tall strikers were signed to *complement* [add to] the squad's lightweight playmakers – who could hardly regard it as a *compliment* [statement of approval] to their abilities.

The general told them that mindless bravery was their *core* requirement in battle. Members of the *corps* weren't too impressed.

Mary was happy to join the local *council*, but she hoped someone would *counsel* [advise] her on what she had to do.

Gordon took his boss's comment as a *cue* to ask for promotion. He joined a long *queue* of applicants.

Louise tossed her *currant* bun over the side. It was carried away by the *current*, and its *current* [present] address is on the bed of the Atlantic.

The prudent housewife decided not to buy the venison because it was too *dear*. 'Yes, madam, it is a little *deer*,' the butcher joked.

Past and present

Quite a few homonyms are produced by the -ed endings of verbs in the past tense, and if you're stuck between two possible spellings it can be useful to consider whether the one you want is an 'action' word.

Was the rogue organisation band *or* banned*? Yes, it's a verb (*to ban*), so it's the -ed ending you want. (A* band *is, of course, a group of musicians.)*

Here are some other examples, with the verb on the right of each pair:

aloud	*allowed*
bald	*bawled*
bold	*bowled*
brood	*brewed*
build	*billed*
chaste	*chased*
crude	*crewed*
duct	*ducked*
find	*fined*
guest	*guessed*
mind	*mined*
mist	*missed*

54

ode (poem)	owed
pact	packed
past	passed
paste	paced
side	sighed
sword	soared
tide	tied
toad	towed
trust	trussed

As ever, there are exceptions to the rule. The past tense of to lay *is* laid *rather than 'layed' and, similarly, you* pay *today and you* paid *yesterday. (Life is tough.)*

The present tense with its -s endings also throws up a few homonyms. The book lacks *or* lax *clarity? The verb is* to lack, *so that's the one to plump for. (*Lax *means 'careless'.)*

Other examples:

bruise	brews
fleas (insects)	flees (runs away)
freeze/frieze	frees
size	sighs

Whether or not he came was *dependent* upon the weather. It all hung upon that.
If he did come, he would bring his *dependants* – two sons and a daughter.

Before I should *die* (and *dying*'s no 'if'),
I'd like some blond *dye*stuff for *dyeing* my quiff.

She was always *discreet* [tactful], and knew better than to blurt out what she knew about her friends.
But she divided them into two *discrete* [separate] groups – those who would be upset if she blabbed, and those who would relish the drama.

One of them tried to *elicit* [coax out] gossip from her, especially about shamefully *illicit* [illegal or underhand] affairs.

He had been given a *faint* [slight] chance of winning the bout, but a *feint* [dummy move] with his left followed by an uppercut with his right gave him the title on a knockout.

The *fair* was held on a *fair*, sunny day, as Jimmy thought only *fair*.
After all, the train *fare* to get there had been expensive, and he had to pay for the crisps, sandwiches and other *fare* on offer.

56

Getting there on time had been quite a *feat*, even though he hadn't come on his own two *feet*.

The flower arrangers showed great *flair* [style or imagination] by matching the size and colour of their blooms.
The orange of the irises seemed to *flare* [blaze] brightly like a flame.

Mix *flour* and butter to make your pastry.
(Your skills will *flower* if you follow my recipes.)

Go *forth* and multiply, birth after birth,
But stop at the *fourth* or we'll ruin the earth.

The weather was *foul* for the human race, but ideal for ducks and other water*fowl*.

Martha claimed to suffer from an existential angst programmed in the womb by her *genes*.
Doubters found her carefully slit *jeans* far more distressed.

There was a brisk market in *gilt*-edged securities. Johnson had *guilt* feelings about not having advised his clients to buy any.

The hairy *gorilla* in its cage practised *guerilla* tactics, rushing out to attack the other apes.

It can *grate* on the ear to hear a stick being scraped along the bars of an iron *grate*.
In these cases it's *great* to wear earplugs.

One can only utter a *groan* when watching politicians kissing babies.
Let them try kissing *grown*-ups instead and then see what happens.

He ordered another glass and said it was the *hair* of the dog.
The dog couldn't catch the rabbit, so chased a *hare* instead.

There's none so deaf as those who will not *hear*.
There's none of us who can't learn spelling *here*.

The workmen spent ages digging a *hole* before filling it in again.
Keeping them occupied for a *whole* month was apparently the sole object of the exercise.

The *holy* man said his prayers five times a day.
He was *wholly* preoccupied with his religion.

The devil finds work for *idle* hands to do.
In her youth she had been a matinée *idol* [person excessively adored or admired].

58

The dreaded apostrophe

It's such a lovely day that even the gloomiest Eeyore of a donkey is swishing *its* tail.

Pet peeve

There's no getting away from it: the apostrophe is prime peeve territory. Good people have missed out on jobs and university places by erroneously putting it in or leaving it out.

The norm is to use an apostrophe to show possession: father's temper, Aunt Mabel's surgical stockings, the ocean's currents and so on. You might logically conclude that a donkey ought to swish it's *tail — but you'd be horribly wrong.*

The problem is that the apostrophe is needed to play another role: the little mark shows that letters are missing, or 'elided': I've *for* I have, *for instance, and* we're *for* we are.

Our grammatical lords and masters have decreed that the apostrophe in it's *is reserved for this second use. So* it's *is short for* it is *or* it has. *Exclusively. Turn the page, and we'll go over that again.*

***It's** always means* it is *or* it has.

It's *a fine day.* It's *been great knowing you.* It's *a mistake we all make through carelessness, even when we know the rule.*

And of course, if we're reserving the apostrophe solely for elision (leaving letters out), it follows that the possessive form of its *never has one.*

The possessive form is always *its*.

The tree is shedding its *leaves, the snake is shedding* its *skin, this book is driving* its *readers close to madness.*

And another thing...

Pet peeve

While we're on the subject of elision, please note an absolute mega-peeve which has crept into blogs, emails and all the other unedited online outlets in recent years: 'could of', 'should of' and 'would of'. The problem this time is the little 'schwa' sound that we met on page 20. What people are hearing is the elided version of could have, should have *and* would have. *They should be writing* could've, should've *and* would've.

Elision fields

Many elided forms sound like other words, and the trick is to recognise the words that need the apostrophe in them. Here's a sample. In each case, the apostrophe denotes that letters have been omitted.

he'd	(he did/would)	heed
I'll	(I will/shall)	aisle, isle
let's	(let us)	(holiday) lets
there's	(there is/has)	theirs (no apostrophe!)
we'd	(we had/would)	weed
we'll	(we will/shall)	wheel
we're	(we are)	weir
we've	(we have)	weave
you'll	(you will/shall)	yule
you're	(you are)	your, (days of) yore

Note the difference between who's *(who is/who has) and* whose *(belonging to whom):*

Who's *the man* whose *shoes are in the news?*

And especially beware their, there *and* they're:

Their *prize courgettes are over* there, *and* they're *the biggest I've ever seen.*

It was of *key* importance, Martin told the other directors, that he should have the *key* to the safe. They resented the fact that he could afford a luxury yacht moored down at the *quay*.

It's true that the baker we watched *knead* his bread was knock-*kneed*, but there really was no *need* to comment on it.

One thing I *knew* and *know* for sure:
A *new* broom spares *no* dirty floor.

That *knot* you just tied is a granny.
It's *not* likely to do the job.

Ancient water pipes were made of *lead*.
They *led* to widespread poisoning.
(But note that in the present tense they still *lead* to poisoning if they're not replaced.)

The football ground was *leased* to the club for a million pounds a year.
The owner said it was the *least* he could charge.

Good behaviour will *lessen* your chance of imprisonment – a useful *lesson* to learn.

The bank manager refused me a *loan*.
He said he preferred working couples as clients rather than a *lone* individual.

He asked why his hotel bed hadn't been *made*.
A *maid* rushed upstairs with fresh sheets.

She said she was sickened by the kind of stuff that had arrived in the *mail*.
He assured her that it was just a *male* thing.

Sales day at the *mall* was a terrifying experience. Frenzied shoppers started to *maul* one another like wild animals.

Sally decided to give up *meat* and to cook only vegetables for any new friend she should *meet*. Hungry Bob thought this was only to *mete* out punishment, so he made his excuses and left.

The tribesmen made weapons of solid *metal*, then showed their pluck and *mettle* [courage] by using them to hunt wild animals.

The *miner* fell heavily in the pit, but luckily suffered only *minor* injuries.

It was early *morning* at the crematorium when the bereaved family arrived in deep *mourning*.

Why was the *naval* officer shy with women?
Because his torso bore a colourful birthmark close to his *navel*.

They managed to score only *one* goal.
Fortunately they *won* the game with it.

The injury caused her great *pain*.
She had smashed her hand through the window *pane*.

She bought a *pair* of knives.
One was to *pare* the skin off an apple, the other to cut a Conference *pear* in half.

The only way to broker *peace* between the two countries was to divide the *piece* of land which lay between them.

Once the mountaineer had scaled the *peak*, he raised his binoculars to take a *peek* over the other side.
Seeing that the other team had got there first, he snapped his flagpole in half in a fit of *pique*.

He meant to *pedal* home as fast as he could, but a salesman with a suitcase stood in the path of his bicycle, trying to *peddle* [sell] brushes and dusters.

A fishy *reek* assailed his nostrils from the keepnet.
Meanwhile, a passing pike began to *wreak* havoc with the smaller fish in the river.

Having taken a *rest*, the *rest* of the army began a campaign to *wrest* control of the country from the enemy.

The sick man began to *retch* into a bucket.
The poor *wretch* had been ill for weeks.

He gave her a *ring* to apologise.
She felt as though she'd like to *wring* his neck.

His new *rôle* was as a stand-up comedian.
The audience would *roll* around in the aisles.

The *root* cause of our getting lost was a faulty GPS.
We ended up adding 50 miles to our *route*.

The old-fashioned way to learn spelling was by *rote* learning.
Unfortunately, the endless repetition didn't always improve what people *wrote*.

Our yacht needed a new *sail*.
We bought one at a car-boot *sale*.

Soon we shall put out to *sea* again, and we hope to *see* places we have never visited before.

His trousers have come apart at the *seams*.
It *seems* that he's wearing scarlet underpants.

His wife will *sew* them up *so* that his modesty is preserved.
It might *sow* the seeds of a better relationship.

There is no finer *sight* than the Grand Canyon. Tourists often *cite* [mention] it as one of the most magical *sites* [places] they've been to.

Prices will *soar* when supplies are low.
The public feel *sore* about that.

Spelling trivia

- Rhythms *is the longest English word not to contain any of the basic five vowels.*

- *The longest palindromes (words which read the same in both directions) are* deified, reviver *and* rotator.

- Underground *and* underfund *are the only words that begin and end with the letters 'und'.*

We hear a creak upon the *stair*
And start to *stare* – is someone there?

If so, she's stopped moving and is *stationary*.
Perhaps it's Aunt Mary coming down to find pen, paper and other *stationery*.

She doesn't have to *steal* them.
All she needs is to *steel* herself to ask.

You don't have to believe his *story*, but he claims to have survived a fall from the top of a nine-*storey* building.

He says he was in the honeymoon *suite*.
Did his *sweet*heart push him?

He was saved when the *tail* of his dinner jacket caught in the window catch.
Well, that's his *tale* anyway.

I was poorly *taught* at school.
When it came to the exams I was tense and *taut* [anxious; also tight] with worry.

The gardening *team* arrived with spades and hoes.
After careful planting, the plot would *teem* [swarm] with wildlife.

She couldn't help but shed a *tear*.
People were on their feet applauding her in every *tier* [level] of the theatre.

He *threw* the javelin a record-breaking length. Unfortunately it sailed beyond the athletics track and *through* an open window, and everyone heard an awful cry.

Pet peeve

When it's all too much

You're more likely to make this mistake through carelessness than ignorance, but do be aware that it's a peevologist's classic.

- To *is either a part of a verb (*to *wound) or a preposition placed before a noun:* 'He is being taken to the police station.'

- Too *is the word that means 'over the top' or 'as well':* 'These men are simply too officious.' 'Their coach is going with them, too.'

- Two *is the number:* 'There are surely two ways of looking at this, officer.'

His protests were all in *vain*.
The weather *vane* suggested a following wind was to blame, but the javelin had entered a *vein*.

This explained the loud cry, or *wail*.
He wasn't exactly having a *whale* of a time.

Now he could only *wait*, feeling the terrible *weight* of responsibility on his shoulders.

He decided to *waive* [give up] his right to be represented by a solicitor, and managed a limp *wave* to his supporters to reassure them.

The officer had to *warn* him that anything he said might be used in evidence against him. After several hours of questioning he felt quite *worn* out.

He felt *weak* at the knees when they told him he would be held for a *week*.

He was given prison overalls to *wear*. *Where* were they going to take him?

They repeatedly *wheeled* him in for more questioning.
Why had he wanted to *wield* a javelin in the first place?

71

They asked him *whether* he really blamed the *weather*.

After a *while* it was all over, but he'd had to use every trick and *wile* [craftiness] to convince them.

The crushed dog gave a mighty *whine*.
The crushed grape gave a little *wine*.

Pet peeve

Whose fault is it?

I wonder *who's* coming to the party.
Perhaps the girl *whose* invitation I delivered myself.

• Who's *is an elision of* who is *or* who has: *Who's (who is) the girl with the purple wig? Who's (who has) been eating all the pies?*

• Whose *is a possessive form (like* its): *This is the girl* whose *perfume drives me insane. This is the guy* whose *flat has been trashed by the partygoers.*

Unless you mean 'who is' or 'who has', always use *whose*.

The cost of bad spelling

In 2011 a British online entrepreneur claimed that spelling mistakes were costing companies a fortune in lost revenue.

Charles Duncombe, whose own websites covered travel, mobile phones and clothing, warned that potential customers judged a site's reliability within seconds – and that bad spelling drove many people away.

He measured the revenue per visitor from one sample site and found that it was twice as high once an error had been corrected. Projected across the whole of Internet retail, this suggested that business worth millions of pounds was being lost every week.

I'm sure I've seen *you* before.

Yes, it was under the *yew* tree over there. Two cows and a *ewe* [female sheep] were eating the grass – until you clapped and they made a *U*-turn.

You say potato...

It was, allegedly, George Bernard Shaw who declared that 'England and America are two countries separated by a common language' – a witty remark, but a gross exaggeration.

Of course, the Americans and the British sometimes use different terms for the same thing (a *sidewalk* for a *pavement*, for example, and *pants* for *trousers*), and their accents are certainly distinct (although there's a great deal of variety within each linguistic culture), but the spelling differs only in a few relatively minor ways which are easy to learn.

We all know the George and Ira Gershwin lyrics:

   You like potayto and I like potahto,
   You like tomayto and I like tomahto . . .

but, on the whole, we find much the same vegetables appearing on both our shopping lists.

The gentle revolution in American spelling was brought about by Noah Webster, a teacher from Connecticut who published *The American Spelling Book* (popularly known as 'the Blue-Backed Speller') in 1783 and *An American Dictionary of the English Language* in 1828.

The former colony had won independence from Britain shortly before his spelling book appeared, and his view was that a national language was 'a band of national union'. The newly independent nation needed a new system 'in language as well as government'.

Webster regarded many of his country's inherited spellings as 'absurd'. Surely *phlegm* should become 'flem', *debt* 'det' and *rough* 'ruf'. As we now know, he had no luck with these.

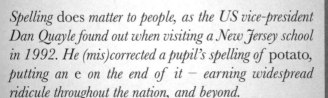

Dan's hot potatoe

Spelling does *matter to people, as the US vice-president Dan Quayle found out when visiting a New Jersey school in 1992. He (mis)corrected a pupil's spelling of* potato, *putting an* e *on the end of it – earning widespread ridicule throughout the nation, and beyond.*

And we might ask, a little cheekily, why he didn't suggest removing the second, unpronounced *c* from his home state of Connecticut.

Webster did, however, introduce changes which, thanks to the later emergence of the United States as a major power, have spread around the world – especially in cyberspace. In the UK we listen to radio *programmes* but use *programs* on our computers. An older generation brought up on *discs* has now succumbed to the arrival of *disks*.

Pet peeve

For the wary speller, the trick is to recognise the differences between the two systems and to be consistent. A peevologist will jump on an American usage which appears out of nowhere in a British English text – and vice versa.

A cautionary tale

The word niggardly *is of Scandinavian origin and means 'miserly'. Although it's spelled with an* a, *the 'schwa' sound in the middle has led some hearers to imagine that it's related to another word that most people find offensive. In 1999 an aide to the mayor of Washington, DC felt obliged to resign after using it – and ever since there's been a reluctance to say it publicly.*

We've covered the use of *-ise/-ize* and *-ice/-ise* on pages 42–44. Here are a few more transatlantic divergences.

Double consonants

American spellers generally do away with the British double *l* before a suffix:

British	*American*
cancelled	canceled
counsellor	counselor
cruellest	cruelest
equalling	equaling
fuelling	fueling
labelled	labeled
modelling	modeling
quarrelled	quarreled
signalling	signaling
traveller	traveler
travelling	traveling

So why does American English retain the double consonant in the likes of *compelled*, *excelling* and *rebelling*? Because the stress falls on those syllables and we'd be pronouncing them 'compeeled', etc., according to the long and short vowel rules. Note that the stress of *labeled* and *modeling* in the above list is safely distant, on the first syllable.

Here, by contrast, are a few words which the British restrict to one *l* while our overseas cousins prefer two:

British	American
appal	appall
enrol	enroll
fulfil	fulfill
instal	install
skilful	skillful
wilful	willful

-our, -or

A familiar across-the-pond difference is the change of an unstressed *-our* in British English (*colour*) to a simple *-or* (*color*). Here are a few more:

British	American
flavour	flavor
harbour	harbor
honour	honor
humour	humor
labour	labor
neighbour	neighbor
rumour	rumor

But when the syllable carries a secondary stress (as in *contour, troubadour*) the two systems converge.

Webster was instrumental in establishing the *-or* form as the American norm *(glamour* is an exception), but as usual there were historical forces at play. In England, the *-our* ending reflected words entering the language from Old French, while *-or* was used for later borrowings direct from Latin. (In British English, *-our* is retained in, for example, *neighbourhood* and *humourless*, but gives way to *-or* in front of some Latin suffixes, as in *honorary, vigorous* and *humorous*.)

-re, -er

Here's another telltale guide to a writer's origins. A good many words in British English retain a French-influenced *-re* ending, as in *fibre*, where the New World prefers the more logical *-er*. A few to look out for:

British	American
calibre	caliber
centre	center
litre	liter
lustre	luster
meagre	meager
metre	meter
ochre	ocher
sombre	somber
theatre	theater

Tidying up

And then take a look at *manoeuvre/maneuver*. Here
we find not only the change of *-re* to *-er* but a
typical piece of American spring cleaning. In
fact, the only wonder is that we haven't ended
up with 'manuver'. In England a man may
grow a *moustache*, but his equally hairy American
friend is reduced to a *mustache*.

British English has a veritable armoury of
words containing the vowels *ae* and *oe* – many
once squeezed together to make the 'ligatures'
æ and œ – which the Americans in their wisdom
have reduced to a single *e*:

British	*American*
amoeba	ameba
anaemia	anemia
archaeology	archeology (sometimes)
diarrhoea	diarrhea
faeces	feces
foetus	fetus
oesophagus	esophagus
oestrogen	estrogen
orthopaedic	orthopedic
paediatric	pediatric

-ogue, -og

Webster stopped short of chopping the end off words such as *catalogue*, but later simplifiers of American spelling weren't at all squeamish about it. *Analog* is the usual US spelling of *analogue*. However, there are many other words, such as *dialogue* and *monologue*, in which most Americans retain the longer spelling.

We'd argue in conclusion that neither system is superior to the other – but would repeat that you need to know the differences between them and should try not to mix them up.

Would you Googol it!

The best-known word in the world of new media is a spelling mistake. The founders of Google thought they'd chosen as their trademark the mathematical term for the number one followed by a hundred zeroes. They were notoriously bad spellers, however, and found out – when it was far too late – that the word they'd been searching for was googol.

The choice is yours

Within British English itself there are quite a few words which have alternative 'correct' spellings. Newspapers, publishers and the legal profession produce style guides to bring a useful uniformity to their own field. These may include such niceties as the position of commas and when to use upper- and lower-case letters, but spelling is always a major concern.

In informal writing it really doesn't matter whether you refer to the juicy fruits as *mangoes* or *mangos*, but if you're about to launch a magazine for your local food marketing board it's a good idea to make an early decision about it, as your readers may find any inconsistency irritating – and perhaps (unreasonably) question your *judgement* or *judgment*.

Here we bring you a ragbag of words for which you can toss a coin. Don't expect a simple logic to apply: the plural of *hoof* may sometimes be found as *hooves*, but a skyscape of *roofs* may never be described as *rooves*. (No, we don't know why.)

acknowledgement	acknowledgment
ageing	aging
amok	amuck
appendices	appendixes
banjos	banjoes
biased	biassed
by-election	bye-election
bylaw	byelaw
carcass	carcase
coloration	colouration
dispatch	despatch
dreamed	dreamt
drier	dryer
drily	dryly
dwarfs	dwarves
encyclopaedia	encyclopedia
enquire	inquire
flamingoes	flamingos
focused	focussed
gaol	jail
gipsy	gypsy
hoofs	hooves
judgement	judgment
kneeled	knelt
liquefy	liquify
lovable	loveable
mileage	milage
moneyed	monied
mottoes	mottos

moveable	movable
nosy	nosey
pricy	pricey
spelled	spelt
swap	swop
tsar	czar
verandah	veranda
wagon	waggon

Note that one pair which doesn't appear above is *all right/alright*. It's likely that this prejudice will eventually be overturned by common usage, but you should be aware that *alright* is regarded in the peevology community as slovenly and deserving of a thwack around the head with a weighty dictionary. And writing *alot* as one word is entirely beyond the pale.

Spelling trivia

- *The commonest letter in English is* e.

- *More words in English begin with an* s *than with any other letter.*

- *The longest word containing no repeated letters is* uncopyrightable.

Talking of dictionaries, we're pleased to present, as our final offering, a compendium of the toughest words in the language – those that time and again crop up in lists of spellings people find most difficult.

With luck, the lessons learned in our little guide will make a trip to these back pages less frequent as time goes by, but don't be ashamed of looking things up – even celebrated writers have their tussles with the language.

'There isn't a man,' fumed Mark Twain, 'who doesn't have to throw out about fifteen hundred words a day when he writes his letters because he can't spell them! It's like trying to do a St. Vitus dance with wooden legs.'

And his fellow countryman H. L. Mencken thought spelling 'one of the arts that are far more esteemed by schoolma'ams than by practical men, neck-deep in the heat and agony of the world'.

Reality cheque

Computer spellcheckers should be avoided by anyone not proficient enough to pick up their crass second-guesses. Within the European Union, translators refer to such errors as 'Cupertinos', because a clumsy keying of the word cooperation *is apt to throw up the name of this Silicon Valley city:* 'The Cupertino *with our Italian comrades,' reads one example, 'proved to be very fruitful.'*

More embarrassing for all concerned was a wild computer shot at the technical word cumulation*: 'The Western Balkan countries . . . requested that they be included in the pan-European system of diagonal* copulation*.'*

One ignorant computer program evidently failed to recognise the Italian word prosciutto*. An online recipe advised cooks to 'crumble bread sticks into a mixing bowl. Cover with warm water. Let soak for 2 to 3 minutes or until soft. Drain. Stir in* prostitute *. . .'*

Using the Latin phrase sua sponte *('of one's own volition') in an American legal document was asking for trouble: 'An appropriate instruction limiting the judge's criminal liability in such a prosecution', the court learned, 'must be given* sea sponge *. . .'*

Practical men and women like Mencken can save their precious time by consulting our *Who's Afraid?* tough words list. Happy spelling!

abbreviate
aberrant
accessible
accommodate
accumulate
ache
achieve
acquiesce
acquire
advice *(noun)*
advise *(verb)*
aggressive
aisle
allotted
allowed *(permitted)*
aloud *(clearly heard)*
anaesthetic
ancient
annihilate
anonymous
answer
antediluvian
apparently
appearance

argument
assassination
autumn
balloted
basically
beautiful
beginning
believe
bigoted
bizarre
business
calendar
calibre
Caribbean
caricature
catalogue
cemetery
census
centre
changeable
charisma
chauffeur
chorus
chrome

colleague
collectible
commission
committed
committee
completely
condemn
conferred
conscience
conscious
consensus
councillor *(politician)*
counsellor *(adviser)*
curiosity
cynic
debt
definitely
dependant *(noun)*
dependent *(adjective)*
desert *(arid area)*
desperate
dessert *(pudding)*
develop
dialogue
diarrhoea
dilemma
disappearance
disappoint

discipline
discreet *(careful)*
discrete *(separate)*
doubt
drunkenness
ecstasy
embarrass
environment
exceed
exhilarate
existence
exorbitant
facial
Fahrenheit
fascinate
fiery
finally
fluorescent
foreign
foreseeable
foreword *(in a book)*
forfeit
forty
forward *(up front)*
fracas
friend
gauge
gist

glamorous
government
guarantee
guard
happened
harass, harassment
hiccough (or hiccup)
hierarchy
honorary
humorous
idiosyncrasy
immediately
incidentally
independent
indict
indispensable
initial
interrupt
irresistible
island
jewellery
knowledge
knuckle
laugh
liaise, liaison
library
licence *(noun)*
license *(verb)*

lore *(tradition)*
maintenance
manageable
manoeuvre
meagre
memento
meter *(measuring device)*
metre *(unit of length)*
millennium
miniature
minuscule
mischievous
misspell
mnemonic
mortgage
muscle
necessary
neighbour
noticeable
obscene
occasion
occurred
occurrence
offered
official
opaque
owe
palatial

A few of your own

We all have our individual spelling hang-ups, so here's a space for you to make a list of words that don't appear in these pages but constantly trip you up…

parallel
pastime
pavilion
peaceable
peculiar
perceived
permissible
persistent
personnel
pharaoh
physique
piece
pneumatic
possession
practice *(noun)*
practise *(verb)*
precede *(go before)*
preferred
prejudice
prestigious
principal *(chief)*
principle *(rule)*
privilege
proceed *(go ahead)*
proffered
pronunciation
propaganda
psychology

publicly
pursue
questionnaire
quiet *(hush)*
quite *(fairly/entirely)*
receipt, receive
recognise
referee
referred, referring
relevant
religious
remember
repetition
resistance
restaurant
rhyme
rhythm
schedule
scissors
seize
separate
siege
similar
skilful
sombre
sophisticated
stationary *(still)*
stationery *(paper etc.)*

subtle	traceable
successful	truly
supersede	twelfth
surprise	typical
syllable	tyranny
tattoo	unforeseen
tendency	unfortunately
theatre	until
therefore	vacuum
thorough	weir
threshold	weird
tomorrow	whistle
tongue	wilful

The last word . . .

Thumb through a dictionary to the very last entry and you may find that it's zymurgy *(the art of fermentation),* Zyrian *(a language spoken in parts of Russia) or* zythum *(a beer made by the ancient Egyptians), but the champion sign-off word is* Zyzzyra *(a genus of tropical American weevils).*

It features in the official Scrabble dictionary, although you'd need a couple of (scoreless) blank tiles along with the single available z *to produce it. But what a way to impress your friends!*

affix An addition to a stem (see prefix and suffix) to create a new word.

analogy In linguistics, the process by which the spelling of one word mimics another, whether through a real or imagined connection.

consonant A speech sound (*b, d, k,* etc.) which is made by using the tongue, teeth or lips to obstruct the flow of air through the mouth or throat.

diacritic A mark, such as an acute accent (*é*) or a tilde (*ñ*), to indicate a change in the pronunciation of a letter.

digraph A combination of two letters representing one sound, as in so*ng*, *ph*one, m*ea*t, bl*oo*d. A digraph is 'split' if it consists of two vowel letters separated by a consonant, as in n*i*c*e* or pl*a*t*e*.

diphthong A combination of two different vowel sounds within the same syllable, as in 'g*ao*l' or 'br*ow*n'; also known as a 'gliding vowel'.

elision The leaving out of one or more letters, usually indicated by an apostrophe, as in *can't* and *isn't*.

etymology The study of the way in which words have changed their form and meaning through history.

homonyms Words (such as *bear* meaning 'carry' and *bear* meaning an animal) which are spelled and pronounced the same but have different meanings.

homophones Words (such as *flour/flower*) which sound the same but are spelled differently.

93

morpheme The smallest grammatical unit in a language.

orthography The standardised form of spelling to represent a given language.

phoneme The basic unit of a language's sound system.

prefix An affix placed in front of a stem word, as in *un*happy, *mis*place.

Received Pronunciation (RP) The standard accent of spoken English, as opposed to local forms.

Romance languages Those modern languages derived from Latin, the major ones being Italian, French, Spanish and Portuguese.

schwa The indistinct vowel sound appearing in unstressed syllables in a great many English words.

Shavian Relating to the works and linguistic theories of the dramatist George Bernard Shaw.

silent letters Those which appear in written script but are unpronounced, as in dum*b*, *k*now.

stem The main element of a word, as opposed to a prefix or suffix.

stress The emphasis placed on a syllable in pronunciation, sometimes changing the sound and/or spelling of a word.

suffix An affix placed after a stem: content*ment*.

syllable A small segment of speech, sometimes purely a vowel sound (*eye*) but usually with consonants, too (*fine, flat*).

vowel One of the sounds (represented by the letters *a, e, i, o, u* and sometimes *y*) spoken with an open mouth.

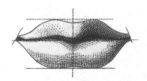